SONGS

THE GREATEST SHOWMAN CAST

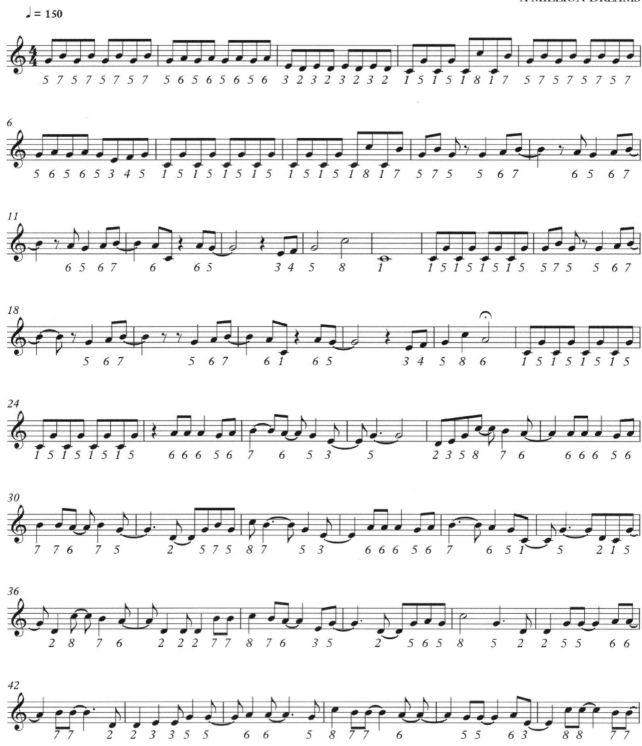

DARKSIDE

ALAN WALKER

WU

ANDY LAU

BEAUTIFUL IN WHITE

WESTLIFE

2

BIG FISH

BEGONIA

9

DANCING ON MY OWN

CALUM SCOTT

10

YOU ARE THE REASON

CALUM SCOTT

2

12

PERFECT

ED SHEERAN

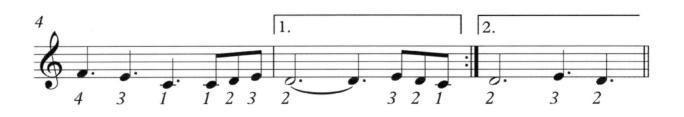

SHAPE OF YOU

ED SHEERAN

CAN'T HELP FALLING IN LOVE

ELVIS PRESLEY

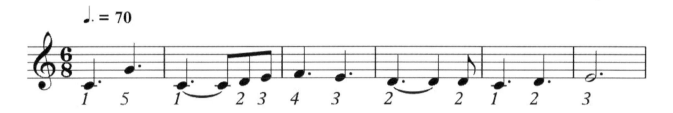

GAME OF THRONES

RAMIN DJAWADI

17

HIDUP INI ADALAH KESEMPATAN

CHRIST IS ENOUGH

HILLSONG

2

20

JU HUA TAI

JAY CHOU

SOLO

JENNIE BLACKPINK

22

23

ONE SUMMER'S DAY

JOE HISAISHI

24

10,000 REASONS

MATT REDMAN

25

TAKE ME TO YOUR HEART

MICHAEL LEAMS TO ROCK

MY HEART WILL GO ON

PIRATES OF THE CARIBBEAN

2

29

RIGHT HERE WAITING FOR YOU

RICHARD MAX

LOSE YOU TO LOVE ME

SELENA GOMEZ

SENORITA

SM&CC

YOU ARE MY SUNSHINE

AMERICAN FOLK SONG

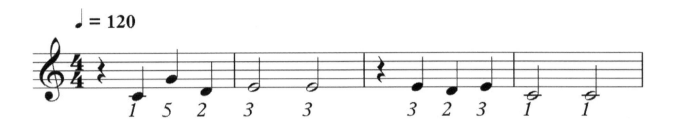

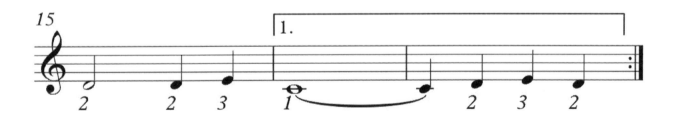

LET HER GO

PASSENGER

SPEAK SOFTLY

ANDY WILLIAMS

THE END OF THE WORLD

SKEETER DAVIS

WE WISH A MERRY CHRISTMAS

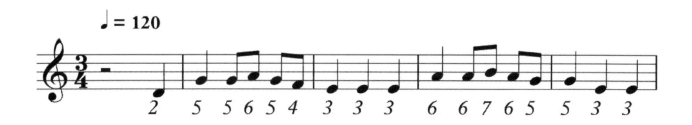

AS THE DEAR

MARTIN NYSTROM

SILENT NIGHT

FRANZ GRUBER

41

Hello there. Thank you for choosing us.

Enjoy the music by hitting the notes.

Surprise Everyone

ALPHA

A R T

Made in United States
Orlando, FL
23 March 2024

45078464R00024